Pond Life

Includes:

What Makes Pond Life Unique?

Habitats and Habits

Bird Activities

Mammal Activities

Fish Activities

Reptile & Amphibian Activities

Invertebrate Activities

Plant Activities

Wildlife Respect

Waterford Press
www.waterfordpress.com

Introduction

More than 100 million ponds can be found in the world. A pond is a body of water that is shallower than a lake. Either natural or artificial, it is usually shallow enough that sunlight reaches the bottom and plants can grow. The deeper the plant roots and the more plants grow in a pond, the water becomes clearer, allowing even more plants to grow and at greater depths. This is a very important part of the pond ecosystem because plants produce more than just food; they produce oxygen in the water. Oxygen in the water is essential to underwater life.

Ponds make excellent freshwater habitats for many types of wildlife, both invertebrate and vertebrate. Some animals, like fish, live in ponds their whole lives, while others, like frogs, spend time there to feed or reproduce. Water birds nest near the pond's edge and feed right from the pond itself. Swimming mammals like shrews and voles build burrows near the water's edge as well. Ponds serve as important havens for other animals to drink fresh water, find cool temperatures or hide from predators (animals who prey on other living things).

Class Act

Animals can be sorted into categories based on certain characteristics. The system for sorting animals into categories is called taxonomy. Mammals, birds, fish, reptiles and amphibians belong to a class of animals called vertebrates. Vertebrates are animals with backbones. Invertebrates are another class of animals that do not have backbones (like insects, worms, snails, lobsters, crabs and spiders).

Draw a line between the animal and its class.

MUD TURTLE

BULLFROG

BLUEGILL

COMMON GALLINULE

MUSKRAT

MAMMAL

BIRD

REPTILE

AMPHIBIAN

FISH

INVERTEBRATE

BLUE-WINGED TEAL

AMERICAN BEAVER

BLACK CRAPPIE

WATER SNAKE

CRAYFISH

SPOTTED SALAMANDER

You Are What You Eat

Herbivores eat mostly plants. Carnivores eat mostly animals.
Omnivores eat plants and animals.

Draw a line between the pond animal and its diet.

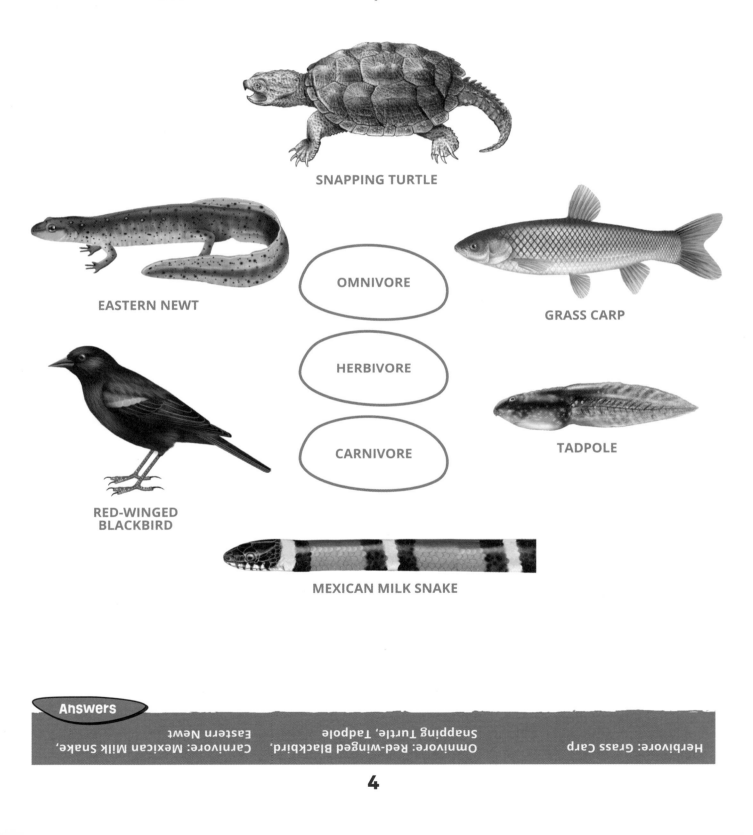

SNAPPING TURTLE

EASTERN NEWT

OMNIVORE

HERBIVORE

CARNIVORE

GRASS CARP

TADPOLE

RED-WINGED
BLACKBIRD

MEXICAN MILK SNAKE

Food Chain

A food chain is the order in which animals feed on other plants or animals.

Producers – A producer takes the sun's energy and stores it as food.

Consumers – A consumer feeds on other living things to get energy. Consumers can include herbivores, carnivores and omnivores.

Decomposers – A decomposer consumes waste and dead organisms for energy.

Label each living organism below as a producer, consumer or decomposer.

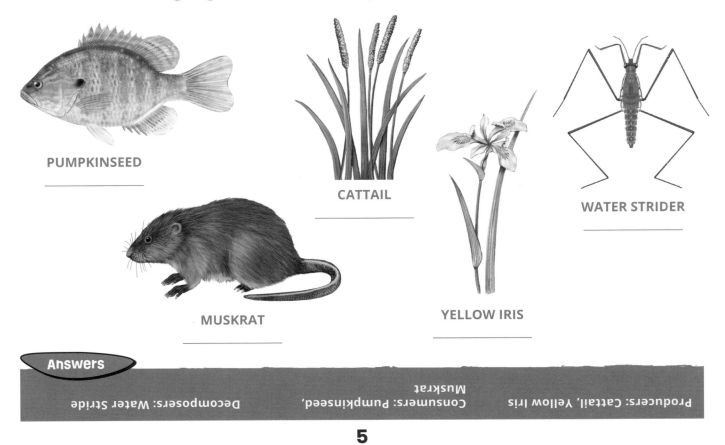

PUMPKINSEED

CATTAIL

YELLOW IRIS

WATER STRIDER

MUSKRAT

Find My Home

There are four distinct habitats in a pond community. Surface film is found at the top, where air-breathing, floating animals like insects live. The open water is home to swimming organisms like fish, microscopic animals and plants that drift in the water. The bottom of ponds is where bottom-feeding fish like catfish or invertebrates like leeches and freshwater mussels live. The shore is where wetland animals like birds, mammals, amphibians and reptiles are found.

Draw a line between the animal and its habitat.

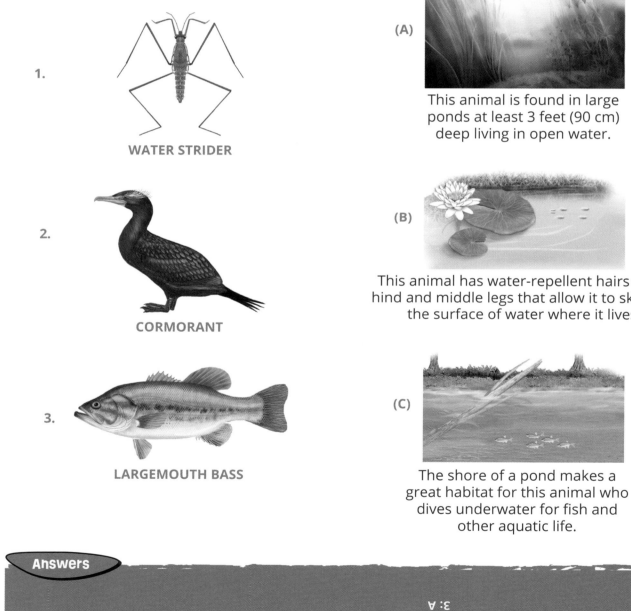

1.

WATER STRIDER

2.

CORMORANT

3.

LARGEMOUTH BASS

(A)

This animal is found in large ponds at least 3 feet (90 cm) deep living in open water.

(B)

This animal has water-repellent hairs on its hind and middle legs that allow it to skate on the surface of water where it lives.

(C)

The shore of a pond makes a great habitat for this animal who dives underwater for fish and other aquatic life.

Name Scramble

A variety of wetland bird species are adapted to living on or near water. "Adapted" means the animal has a body part or behavior that helps it survive better in its environment. Many waterfowl like ducks and geese and several diving and wading birds live near ponds.

Unscramble the letters to form the names of these birds.

1. **LEPCIAN**

2. **NSAW**

3. **OGSOE**

4. **RGEET**

5. **ROHNE**

6. **LUGL**

7. **PTINLIA**

8. **OTCO**

What Does it Eat? Tell by its Beak

All birds have one beak, but they have different shapes due to their different needs like diet, the types of nests it builds, or the type of predators it needs to defend against. Bird beaks are categorized by their shape and function. Here are some common beak types found on birds that live or feed near ponds.

Strong Pecking Beaks – Woodpeckers have beaks that are designed to chisel into bark and wood. They use these beaks to create nests and dig insects or grubs out of trees.

Hooked Beaks – Sharp, curved beaks help birds grab and tear meat. These useful beaks allow them to eat various prey, including mammals, fish, reptiles and amphibians.

Straining Beaks – Ducks with flat bills feed primarily on plants that they strain from the water. Most have a comb-like structure at the edge of their beak that acts as a strainer.

Slender Beaks – Ducks with long, slender beaks are adapted for spearing and/or grasping fish.

Draw a line between the bird and its food.

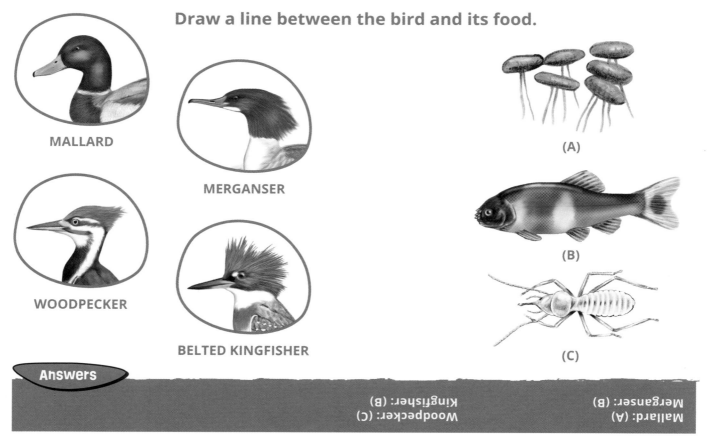

MALLARD

MERGANSER

WOODPECKER

BELTED KINGFISHER

(A)

(B)

(C)

Make Words

Most ducks are known for their long migrations, with many traveling hundreds of miles every year.

The **Mallard** is one of the most well-known ducks in the world. The male has brightly colored plumage. It is a dabbling duck, which means that it tips into the water to find food rather than diving under water. It also forages for food on the land near ponds.

How many words can you make from the letters in its name?

_____   _____

_____   _____

_____   _____

_____   _____

_____   _____

_____   _____

Answers

Possible words include: alarm, drama, llama, lard, mall, marl, all, arm, dam, lad, mad, mar, rad, ram, ad, ma.

9

Word Search

Found in and near ponds all around the globe, semiaquatic (living partly in or near water) mammals are some of the most fascinating species that are adapted to freshwater habitats. Though many of them look like each other, there are some ways to tell them apart. The tail is often a distinguishing feature—for instance, a beaver has a wide, flat tail, and a muskrat has a long, rat-like tail. The animal's shape, type of fur and behavior are other great ways to tell these mammals apart.

Find the names of these pond mammals in the puzzle.

DEER MOUSE

NUTRIA

MUSKRAT

VOLE

WATER SHREW

```
S A T R M M K K A A C E C R E E
T C R A C C O O N A M T V T M E
E B S O T I R T T V O L E N U C
W E A R E R N V R R A O O R E M
A R E T D I I I E K O R O M N E
R I W C E W A U V R I K E O C M
N M W I T N E R A V C M D R U V
A U A D H I O D E E R M O U S E
R S T E R R U R B T U A M N R N
O K E R R C O U K W W O I T K A
E R R S I T S V M T L R N M W N
M A S R T A I E R N L R K R E O
E T H E O I R R C L O A E A R U
E T R N R R S B A T M R M I E R
M E E R C C T I O V K R I O E R
A K W R M R U I O W T O R U C O
```

RACCOON

MINK

RIVER OTTER

BEAVER

Answers

```
O C R U O T R O I U R M R W K A
R E O I R K V O I T C C R E M E
R E I M R M T A B S R R N R T E
U R A E O L C R I O E H T E R U
O E R K R L N R E I A T R S A M
N W M N R L T M V S T I S R R E
A K T I O W W K U O C R R E K O
N R N M A U T B R U R R E T S R
E S U O M R E E D O I H D A U A
V U R D M C V A R E N T I W M M
M C O E K I R V U A W E C W I R
E N M O R O K E I I I D T E R A
M E N M O O A R R V N R A E W E
C U N E L O V T T R I T O S B E
E M T V T M A N O O C C A R C T
E E R C E C A A K K M M R T A S
```

10

Make Words

The **Common Raccoon** is easily distinguished by its ringed tail and masked eyes. One of the smartest mammals, it is found in a variety of habitats and is very comfortable living in large urban areas. It has hypersensitive front paws and is often found near ponds because it likes to soak its food underwater before eating it.

How many words can you make from the letters in its name?

_____   _____

_____   _____

_____   _____

_____   _____

_____   _____

_____   _____

_____   _____

Answers

Possible words include: acorn, croon, cocoa, corn, orca, coco, oar, ran, can, car, con, cam, non, ram, noon, mom, moor, cram, moron, moon, room

11

Maze

Ponds make excellent habitats for frogs. One of the most fascinating frogs is the **Wood Frog**. During hibernation (when animals rest in a safe place during winter), the Wood Frog stops breathing and its heart stops beating. More than half of its body may freeze, but a special antifreeze in its cells protects it from harm. This is why Wood Frogs can live farther north than other frogs.

Help this Wood Frog find a place to hibernate for the winter.

ENTER

Origami

Starting with a square piece of paper, follow the simple folding instructions below to create a jumping frog.

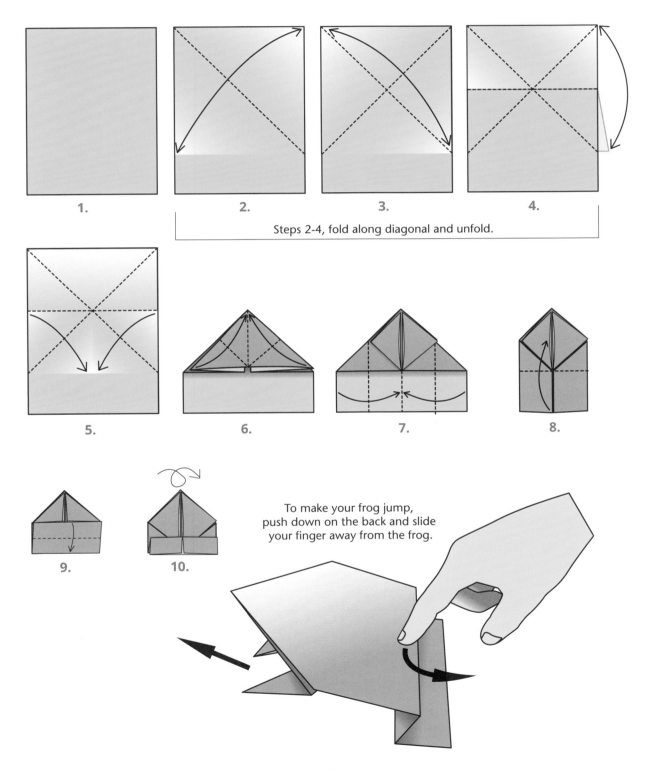

1.

2.

3.

4.

Steps 2-4, fold along diagonal and unfold.

5.

6.

7.

8.

9.

10.

To make your frog jump, push down on the back and slide your finger away from the frog.

Make Words

Salamanders are amphibians. You can often find them in moist areas and under leaf litter in and around ponds. They are unique among vertebrates because of their ability to regenerate lost limbs.

How many words can you make from the letters in its name?

_____   _____

_____   _____

_____   _____

_____   _____

_____   _____

_____   _____

_____   _____

_____   _____

Word Search

Turtles are omnivores that can have a beneficial impact on a pond ecosystem. An ecosystem is a community of living organisms that interact with each other and their environment. Turtles eat plant matter as well as sick and dead fish, keeping ponds clean and reducing the spread of disease. They also help control aquatic weeds and other plants that can cause problems.

Locate these common pond turtles hidden among the letters.

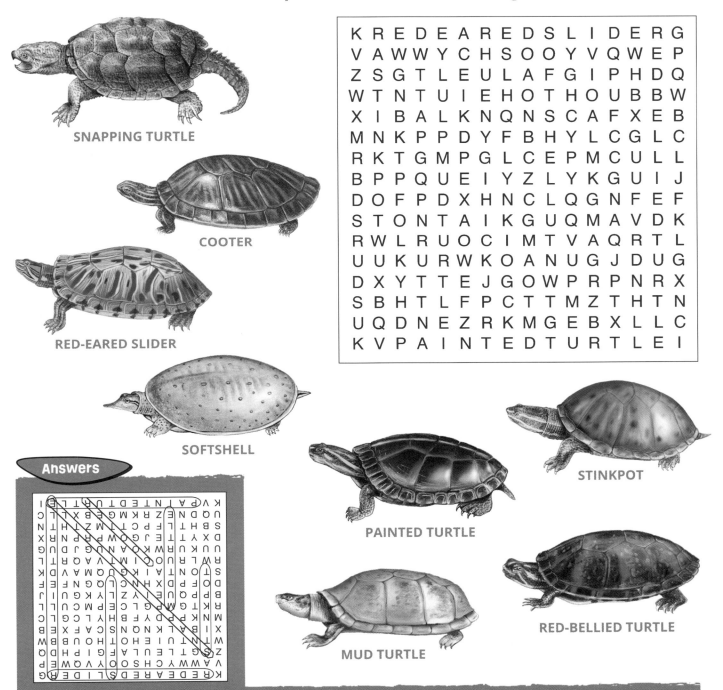

SNAPPING TURTLE

COOTER

RED-EARED SLIDER

```
K R E D E A R E D S L I D E R G
V A W W Y C H S O O Y V Q W E P
Z S G T L E U L A F G I P H D Q
W T N T U I E H O T H O U B B W
X I B A L K N Q N S C A F X E B
M N K P P D Y F B H Y L C G L C
R K T G M P G L C E P M C U L L
B P P Q U E I Y Z L Y K G U I J
D O F P D X H N C L Q G N F E F
S T O N T A I K G U Q M A V D K
R W L R U O C I M T V A Q R T L
U U K U R W K O A N U G J D U G
D X Y T T E J G O W P R P N R X
S B H T L F P C T T M Z T H T N
U Q D N E Z R K M G E B X L L C
K V P A I N T E D T U R T L E I
```

SOFTSHELL

Answers

STINKPOT

PAINTED TURTLE

MUD TURTLE

RED-BELLIED TURTLE

Connect the Dots

Connect the dots in numeric order to reveal a reptile swimming in the pond.

Word Search

Fishes are cold-blooded vertebrates adapted to live in water. They are characterized by their size, shape, feeding habits and water preferences. Most live in either salt water or fresh water, although a few species divide their lives between the two. Ponds are excellent habitats for many freshwater fish species.

Find the names of these common pond fishes in the puzzle.

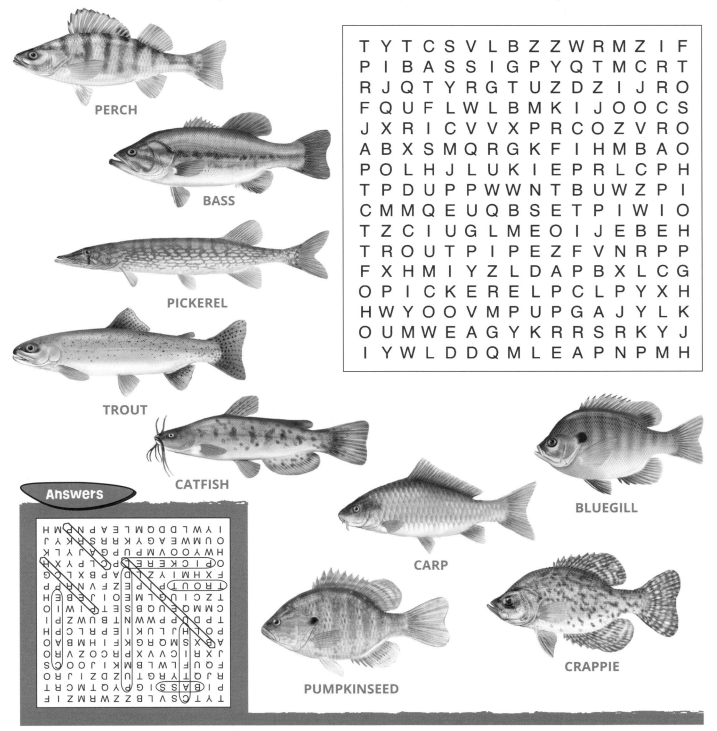

PERCH

BASS

PICKEREL

TROUT

CATFISH

```
T Y T C S V L B Z Z W R M Z I F
P I B A S S I G P Y Q T M C R T
R J Q T Y R G T U Z D Z I J R O
F Q U F L W L B M K I J O O C S
J X R I C V V X P R C O Z V R O
A B X S M Q R G K F I H M B A O
P O L H J L U K I E P R L C P H
T P D U P P W W N T B U W Z P I
C M M Q E U Q B S E T P I W I O
T Z C I U G L M E O I J E B E H
T R O U T P I P E Z F V N R P P
F X H M I Y Z L D A P B X L C G
O P I C K E R E L P C L P Y X H
H W Y O O V M P U P G A J Y L K
O U M W E A G Y K R R S R K Y J
I Y W L D D Q M L E A P N P M H
```

Answers

BLUEGILL

CARP

CRAPPIE

PUMPKINSEED

Spot the Differences

Bluegill is a small fish that is common in ponds throughout North America. It is a common host fish for freshwater mussels that attach themselves to the fish's gills during the larva stage in order to survive. Bluegill are also sometimes called bream, brim, sunny or coppernose.

Can you spot five differences between the fishes below?

Answers

Maze

The **Whirligig Beetle** is a water beetle often seen swimming in circles on the surface of a pond. It has divided eyes that let it see above and below the water.

Help this whirligig spin its way to the center of the pond.

ENTER

Origami

Ladybugs are some of the most effective predatory insects. Predatory means to prey on other living things for food. Ladybugs live in ponds and wetlands and feed on harmful bugs like aphids, mealybugs or mites.

Starting with a square piece of paper, follow the simple folding instructions below to create a ladybug.

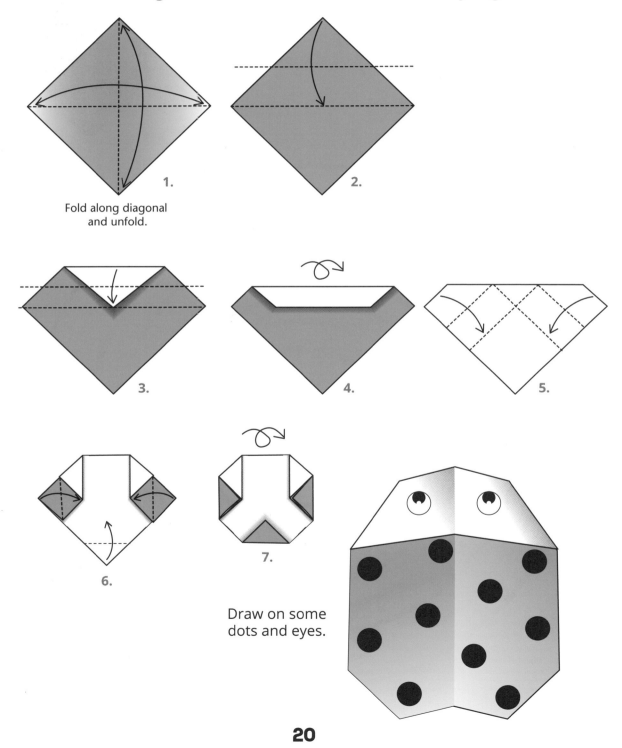

1.

Fold along diagonal and unfold.

2.

3.

4.

5.

6.

7.

Draw on some dots and eyes.

Be an Artist

Draw this crayfish by copying one square at a time.

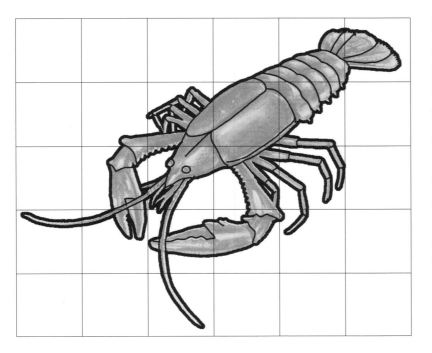

Crayfish are freshwater crustaceans that resemble small lobsters. They are found in brooks, streams and ponds and feed on dead and living plants and animals. Most active at night, they hunt for snails, worms, tadpoles, insect larvae and vegetation. During the day, they conceal themselves under hiding spaces like rocks or logs. They are also known as crawfish or crawdads.

Spot the Differences

Water Striders are insects that can walk on water; you often see them "skating" on the surface of ponds. They feed mostly on insects and spiders that fall on to the water's surface.

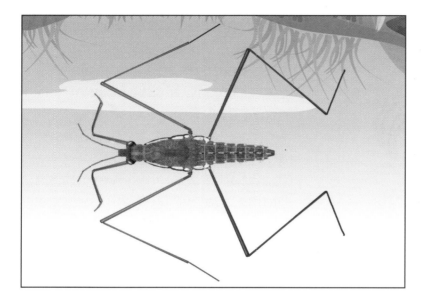

Can you spot five differences between the insects?

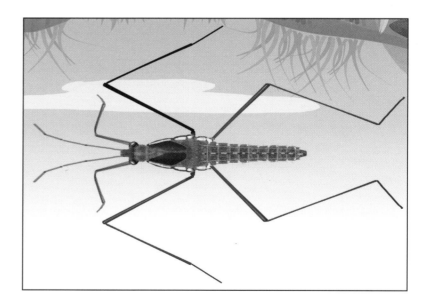

Answers

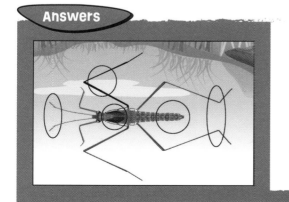

Be an Artist

Draw this dragonfly by copying one square at a time.

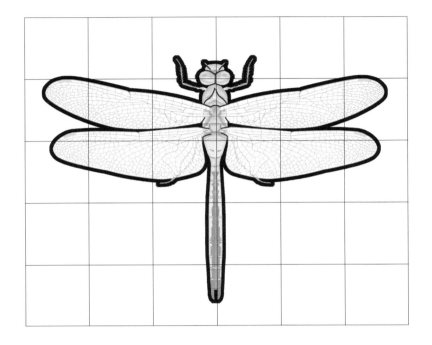

Dragonflies are very impressive fliers. They can fly forward, fly backward, glide and hover. They rest with their wings spread open. Despite their large size and big jaws, they are harmless to humans.

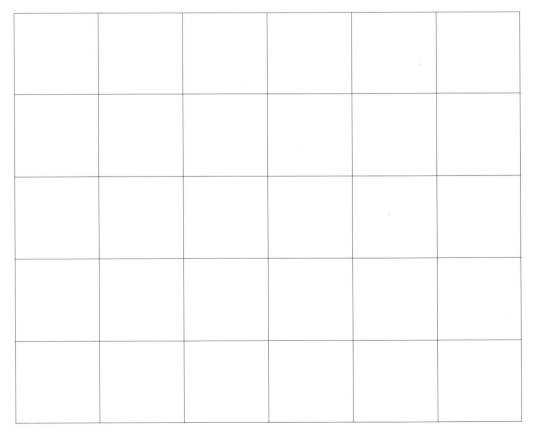

Word Search

Aquatic plants are important to the pond ecosystem. Some grow deep within the water, while some float on the surface. They improve water quality and release oxygen back into the pond.

Find the names of these common pond plants in the puzzle.

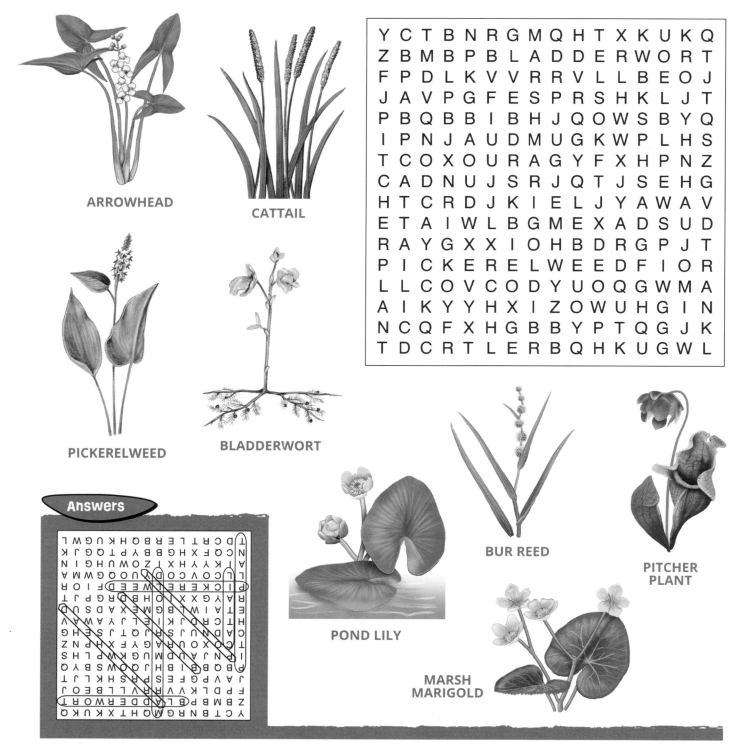

```
Y C T B N R G M Q H T X K U K Q
Z B M B P B L A D D E R W O R T
F P D L K V V R R V L L B E O J
J A V P G F E S P R S H K L J T
P B Q B B I B H J Q O W S B Y Q
I P N J A U D M U G K W P L H S
T C O X O U R A G Y F X H P N Z
C A D N U J S R J Q T J S E H G
H T C R D J K I E L J Y A W A V
E T A I W L B G M E X A D S U D
R A Y G X X I O H B D R G P J T
P I C K E R E L W E E D F I O R
L L C O V C O D Y U O Q G W M A
A I K Y Y H X I Z O W U H G I N
N C Q F X H G B B Y P T Q G J K
T D C R T L E R B Q H K U G W L
```

ARROWHEAD

CATTAIL

PICKERELWEED

BLADDERWORT

Answers

BUR REED

PITCHER PLANT

POND LILY

MARSH MARIGOLD

Name Scramble

Now that you have learned a variety of different species, try some wildlife identification. Identification means to use an animal's characteristics or behaviors to tell what it is.

Unscramble the letters to form the names of these familiar pond animals.

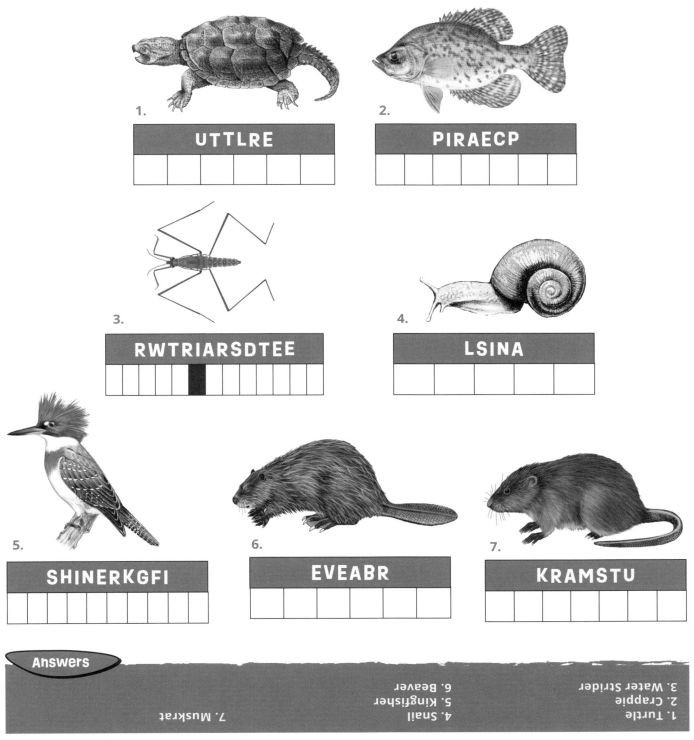

1. UTTLRE

2. PIRAECP

3. RWTRIARSDTEE

4. LSINA

5. SHINERKGFI

6. EVEABR

7. KRAMSTU

Picture Scramble

Place the numbers 1 through 9 in the lettered boxes
on the right to create the image on the left.

BACKSWIMMER

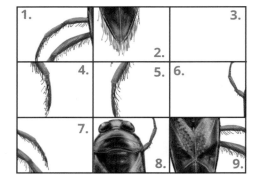

1.   3.
2.
4.   5. 6.
7.
8. 9.

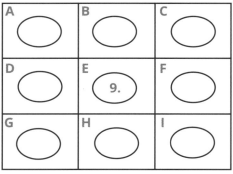

A	B	C
D	E 9.	F
G	H	I

SPRING PEEPER

1. 2. 3.
5.
4. 6.
7. 8. 9.

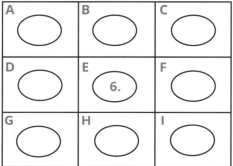

A	B	C
D	E 6.	F
G	H	I

RED MAPLE

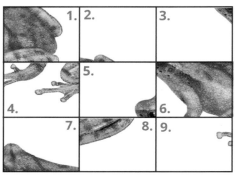

1. 2. 3.
4. 5.
6.
8.
7. 9.

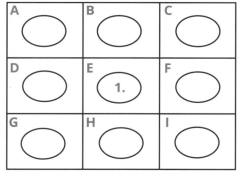

A	B	C
D	E 1.	F
G	H	I

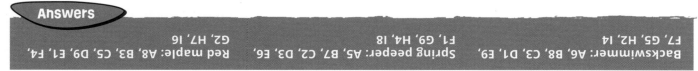

26

Shadow Know-How

Can you name these pond species?

Color Me

Use the Color Keys to help you color the picture of the Monarch and Brook Trout.

Monarch

Color Key

Brook Trout

Color Key

Who Am I?

Name these pond animals by using the clues.

1. I can often be seen scurrying around pond edges looking for food.

_____

2. Unlike frogs, I spend most of my time out of the water hunting for insects and worms to eat.

_____

3. I am a valued pond predator and feed on small insects like mosquitos, flies and ants.

_____

4. I'm a worm-like creature that lives in ponds and feeds on the blood of other animals.

_____

5. I hunt by walking through shallow water making quick jabs at fish and insects.

_____

6. I perch in trees on pond edges and dive into the water to catch fish.

_____

Answers

1. Mouse   2. Toad
3. Dragonfly   4. Leech
5. Heron   6. Kingfisher

Oddball Out

In each row, circle the animal that is different from the others.

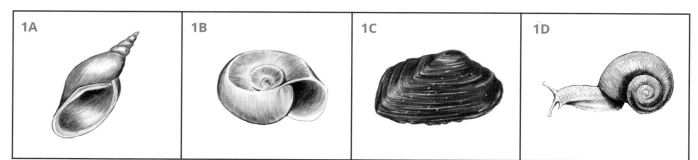

Three of these are snails. Circle the one that is not.

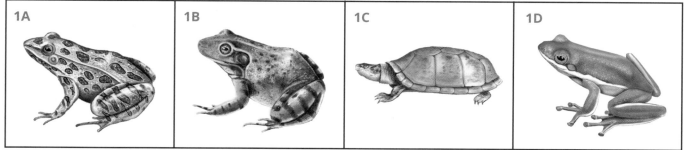

Three of these are frogs. Circle the one that is not.

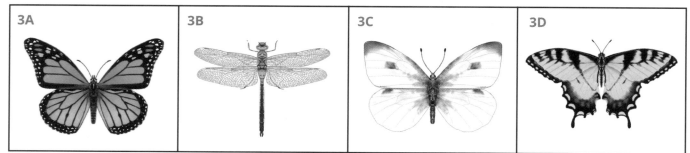

Three of these are butterflies. Circle the one that is not.

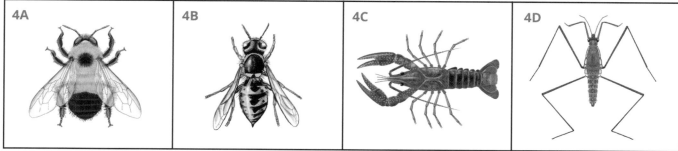

Three of these are insects. Circle the one that is not.